The

Best

Beast

The Best Beast

poems by

Stevie Smith

with drawings by the author

Alfred A. Knopf   New York   1969

We are grateful to Messrs. Longmans Green for permission to
include the following poems from their publication of The Frog Prince:

"The Best Beast of the Fat-Stock Show at Earls Court," "Phèdre,"
"To Carry the Child," "Saffron," "The Frog Prince," "Oh Christianity,
Christianity," "Why do you rage?", "Emily writes such a good
letter," "Easy," "Pretty," "Watchful," "Piggy to Joey," "But
Murderous," "Nodding," "Widowhood or The Home-Coming of Lady
Ross," "Es war einmal," "Is it Happy?", "The Last Turn of the Screw,"
"The Listener," "How Cruel is the Story of Eve," "Anger's Freeing
Power," "The Castle," "The Crown of Gold," "Our Bog is Dood,"
"The Wedding Photograph," "A House of Mercy," "Under Wrong
Trees . . . or Freeing the Colonial Peoples," "Egocentric," "Exeat,"
"A Dream of Comparison," "Northumberland House," "Mrs Arbuthnot,"
"Dear Child of God," "I had a dream . . ."

"O Pug" and "Hippy-Mo" were first published in the New Statesman;
"A Soldier Dear to Us" and "The Ass" in Ambit; *"Oh Grateful*
Colours, Bright Looks" in The Times Literary Supplement;
"Mrs Arbuthnot" in The New York Times; *and "To Carry the*
Child" in The New Yorker.

Contents

The
Best
Beast

The Best Beast of the Fat-Stock Show at Earls Court

(*In monosyllables*)

The Best Beast of the Show
Is fat,
He goes by the lift—
They all do that.

This lift, large as a room,
(Yet the beasts bunch),
Goes up with a groan,
They have not oiled the winch.

Not yet to the lift
Goes the Best Beast,
He has to walk on the floor to make a show
First.

Great are his horns,
Long his fur,
The Beast came from the North
To walk here.

Is he not fat?
Is he not fit?
Now in a crown he walks
To the lift.

When he lay in his pen,
In the close heat,
His head lolled, his eyes
Were not shut for sleep.

Slam the lift door,
Push it up with a groan,
Will they kill the Beast now?
Where has he gone?

When he lay in the straw
His heart beat so fast
His sides heaved, I touched his side
As I walked past.

I touched his side,
I touched the root of his horns;
The breath of the Beast
Came in low moans.

Phèdre

I wonder why Proust should have thought
The lines from Racine's Phèdre
    Depuis que sur ces bords les dieux ont envoyé
    La fille de Minos et de Pasiphaé to be
Entirely devoid of meaning,
To me they seem
As lucid as they are alarming.

I wonder why
The actresses I have seen
Playing Phèdre
Always indulge
In such mature agonising.
Phèdre was young,
(This is as clear in Racine as Euripides)
She was young,
A girl caught in a trap, a girl
Under the enforcement
Of a goddess.
I dare say Phèdre
In fact I'm sure of it
Was by nature
As prim as Hippolytus,
Poor girl, poor girl, what could she do
But be ashamed and hang herself,
Poor girl.

How awful the French actress
Marie Bell
Made her appear.
Poor Phèdre,
Not only to be shamed by her own behaviour,
Enforced by that disgusting goddess,
Ancient enemy
Of her family,
But nowadays to have to be played
By actresses like Marie Bell
In awful ancient agonising, something painful.

Now if I
Had been writing this story
I should have arranged for Theseus
To die,
(Well, *he* was old)
And then I should have let
Phèdre and Hippolytus
Find Aricie out
In some small meanness,
Say
Eating up somebody else's chocolates,
Half a pound of them, soft-centred.
Secretly in bed at night, alone,
One after another,
Positively wolfing them down.
This would have put Hip. off,
And Phèdre would be there too
And he would turn and see
That she was pretty disgusted, too,

So then they would have got married
And everything would have been respectable,
And the wretched Venus could have lumped it,
Lumped, I mean, Phèdre
Being the only respectable member
Of her awful family,
And being happy.

I should have liked one member
Of that awful family
To be happy,
What with Ariadne auf Naxos,
And Pasiphaé and that awful animal,
And Minos sitting judging the Dead
In those awful dark halls.
Yes, I should like poor honourable simple sweet prim Phèdre
To be happy. One would have to be pretty simple
To be happy with a prig like Hippolytus,
But she was simple.
I think it might have been a go,
If I were writing the story
I should have made it a go.

To Carry the Child

To carry the child into adult life
Is good? I say it is not,
To carry the child into adult life
Is to be handicapped.

The child in adult life is defenceless
And if he is grown-up, knows it,
And the grown-up looks at the childish part
And despises it.

The child, too, despises the clever grown-up,
The man-of-the-world, the frozen,
For the child has the tears alive on his cheek
And the man has none of them.

As the child has colours, and the man sees no
Colours or anything,
Being easy only in things of the mind,
The child is easy in feeling.

Easy in feeling, easily excessive
And in excess powerful,
For instance, if you do not speak to the child
He will make trouble.

You would say a man had the upper hand
Of the child, if a child survive?
I say the child has fingers of strength
To strangle the man alive.

Oh it is not happy, it is never happy,
To carry the child into adulthood,
Let children lie down before full growth
And die in their infanthood

And be guilty of no man's blood.

But oh the poor child, the poor child, what can he do,
Trapped in a grown-up carapace,
But peer outside of his prison room
With the eye of an anarchist?

Saffron

Underneath the ice
Lies the frozen spirit of Bice

Green are her eyes, green her hair,
The spirit of Bice is winter's prisoner.

When spring comes Pale is her name, and her hair
And eyes are pale blue, and she is freer.

In summertime she is called Saffron,
Yellow are eyes and hair then. I welcome

Bice, Pale and Saffron but I love best
Beautiful summer Saffron, running fast.

Because this beautiful spirit should not be frozen
And is furthest from it when she is saffron.

A Soldier Dear to Us

It was the War,
I was a child,
They came from the trenches
To our suburb mild.

Our suburb then was more a country place,
They came to our house for release.

In the convalescent army hospital,
That was once a great house and landed estate,
Lay Basil, wounded on the Somme,
But his pain was not now so great

That he could not be fetched in a bath chair,
Or hobble on crutches, to find in our house there
My mother and aunt, his friends on leave, myself, I was twelve,
And a hearthrug to lie down in front of the fire on
                                        and rest himself.

It was a November golden and wet,
As there had been little wind that year and the leaves were yet
Yellow on the great trees, the oak trees and elms,
Of our beautiful suburb as it was then.
When Basil woke up he liked to talk and laugh,
He was a sweet tempered laughing man, he said:
My dear child, listen to this. Then he read
From The Church Times how angry the bishop was because
Of the Reserved Sacrament in the church

Of St. Alban's, Holborn. Now my dear, he said, for a treat
Next Sunday I will take you to All Saints, Margaret Street. Only
You will have to sit on the ladies' side

                  though you're not yet one really.

Basil never spoke of the trenches, but I
Saw them always, saw the mud, heard the guns,

                  saw the duckboards,

Saw the men and the horses slipping into the great mud, saw
The rain fall and never stop falling, saw the gaunt
Trees and the rusty frame
Of the abandoned gun carriages. Because it was the same
As the poem "Childe Roland to the Dark Tower Came"
I was reading at school.

Basil and Tommy and Joey Porteus who came to our house
Were too brave even to ask *themselves* if there was any hope,
So we laughed, as they laughed, as they laughed when Basil said:
What will Ronny do now (it was Ronny Knox) will he pope?
And later, when he had poped, Tommy gave me his book

                  for a present,

The Spiritual Aeneid and I read of the great torment
Ronny had had to decide, Which way, this or that?
But I thought Basil and Tommy and Joey Porteus were

                  more brave than that.

Coming to our house
Were the brave ones, and I could not look at them,
For my strong feelings, except now and then
Slantingly, from the hearth mat, look at them.

Oh Basil, Basil, you had such a merry heart,
But you taught me a secret you did not perhaps mean to impart,
That one must speak lightly, and use fair names like the ladies
They used to call The Eumenides.

Oh Basil, I was a child at school,
My school lessons coloured
My thoughts of you.

ENVOI

Tommy and Joey Porteus were killed in France.

Now fifty years later

Basil has died of the shots he got in the shell crater
The shrapnel has worked round at last to his merry heart,

I write this

For a memorial of the soldier dear to us he was.

The Frog Prince

I am a frog,
I live under a spell,
I live at the bottom
Of a green well.

And here I must wait
Until a maiden places me
On her royal pillow,
And kisses me,
In her father's palace.

The story is familiar,
Everybody knows it well,
But do other enchanted people feel as nervous
As I do? The stories do not tell,

Ask if they will be happier
When the changes come,
As already they are fairly happy
In a frog's doom?

I have been a frog now
For a hundred years
And in all this time
I have not shed many tears,

I am happy, I like the life,
Can swim for many a mile
(When I have hopped to the river)
And am for ever agile.

And the quietness,
Yes, I like to be quiet
I am habituated
To a quiet life,

But always when I think these thoughts
As I sit in my well
Another thought comes to me and says:
It is part of the spell

To be happy
To work up contentment
To make much of being a frog
To fear disenchantment

Says, It will be *heavenly*
To be set free,
Cries, *Heavenly* the girl who disenchants
And the royal times, *heavenly*,
And I think it will be.

Come, then, royal girl and royal times,
Come quickly,
I can be happy until you come
But I cannot be heavenly,
Only disenchanted people
Can be heavenly.

Oh Christianity, Christianity

Oh Christianity, Christianity,
Why do you not answer our difficulties?
If He was God He was not like us,
He could not lose.

Can Perfection be less than perfection?
Can the creator of the Devil be bested by him?
What can the temptation to possess the earth have meant to Him
Who made and possessed it? What do you mean?

And Sin, how could He take our sins upon Him?
What does it mean?

To take sin upon one is not the same
As to have sin inside one and feel guilty.

It is horrible to feel guilty,
We feel guilty because we are.
Was *He* horrible? Did *He* feel guilty?

You say He was born humble—but He was not,
He was born God—
Taking our nature upon Him. But then you say,
He was Perfect Man. Do you mean
Perfectly Man, meaning wholly; or Man without sin? Ah
Perfect Man without sin is not what we are.

Do you mean He did not know that He was God,
Did not know He was the Second Person of the Trinity?

(Oh, if He knew this, and was,
It was a source of strength for Him we do not have)
But this theology of "emptying" you preach sometimes—
That He emptied Himself of knowing He was God—seems
A theology of false appearances
To mock your facts, as He was God (if He was), whether He knew it or not.

Oh what do you mean, what do you mean?
You never answer our difficulties.

You say, Christianity, you say
That the Trinity is unchanging from eternity,
But then you say
At the incarnation He took
Our Manhood into the Godhead,
That did not have it before,
So it must have altered it,
Having it.

Oh what do you mean, what do you mean?
You never answer our questions.

Why do you rage?

Why do you rage so much against Christ, against Him
Before Whom angel brightness grows dark, heaven dim?
Is He not wonderful, beautiful? Is He not Love?
Did He not come to call you from Heaven above?
Say, Yes; yes, He did; say, Yes; call Him this:
Truth, Beauty, Love, Wonder, Holiness.

Say, Yes. Do not always say, No.

Oh I would if I thought it were so,
Oh I know that you think it is so.

Emily writes such a good letter

Mabel was married last week
So now only Tom left.

The doctor didn't like Arthur's cough
I have been in bed since Easter.

A touch of the old trouble.

I am downstairs today.
As I write this
I can hear Arthur roaming overhead.

He loves to roam,
Thank heavens he has plenty of space to roam in.

We have seven bedrooms
And an annexe,

Which leaves a flat for the chauffeur and his wife,

We have much to be thankful for.

The new vicar came yesterday,
People say he brings a breath of fresh air,

He leaves me cold;
I do not think he is a gentleman.

Yes, I remember Maurice very well,
Fancy getting married at his age,
She must be a fool.

You knew May had moved?
Since Edward died she has been much alone,

It was cancer.

No, I know nothing of Maud,
I never wish to hear her name again,
In my opinion Maud
Is an evil woman.

Our char has left
And a good riddance too;
Wages are very high in Bournemouth.

Write and tell me how you are, dear,
And the girls,
Phoebe and Rose;
They must be a great comfort to you,
Phoebe and Rose.

Look!

I am becalmed in a deep sea
And give signals, but they are not answered
And yet I see ships in the distance
And give signals, but they do not answer.

Am I a pariah ship, or a leper,
To be shunned reasonably?
Or did I commit a crime long ago
And have forgotten, but they remember?

Into the dark night to darker I move,
And the lights of the ships are not seen now,
But instead there is a phosphorescence from the water.
That light shines, and now I see

Low down, as I bend my hand in the water,
A fish so transparent in his inner organs
That I know he comes from the earthquake bed,
Five miles below where I sail, I sail.

All his viscera are transparent, his eyes globule on stalks,
Is he dead? Or alive and only languid? Now
Into my hand he comes, the travelling creature,
Not from the sea-bed alone but from the generations,
Faint, because of the lighter pressure,
Fainting, a long fish, stretched out.

So we meet, and for a moment
I forget my solitariness
But then I should like to show him,
And who shall I show him to?

Easy

Easy in their ugly skins
Claudius and Gertrude were,
They *liked* as well as loving each other,
They were a humdrum pair.

Of all the people in that bloodstained play
They are the only ones
Who might have been living today.

Hamlet dimly perceived
They were not entirely of his times.
Their witless freedom of the ages
Irked him sometimes.

He, a man of two times—
His Yesterday, *his* Today—
Could not stretch
To their timelessness,
He was too much on edge.

Banausic, he called them, banausic,
A villainous banausic couple.
He turned to blow on his love for his father
And found it rubble.

Mouthing at Yesterday's ghostly manifestation
A sentence or two from Wittenberg, likely at least
To put a ghost in its place,
He discovered no satisfaction,
And no sense.

Sadly his heart heaved. Where was there a shield for him
Against banausic couples in their ugly skin
Easy, easy? There was never any ease for him.

Pretty

Why is the word pretty so underrated?
In November the leaf is pretty when it falls
The stream grows deep in the woods after rain
And in the pretty pool the pike stalks

He stalks his prey, and this is pretty too,
The prey escapes with an underwater flash
But not for long, the great fish has him now
The pike is a fish who always has his prey

And this is pretty. The water rat is pretty
His paws are not webbed, he cannot shut his nostrils
As the otter can and the beaver, he is torn between
The land and water. Not "torn," he does not mind.

The owl hunts in the evening and it is pretty
The lake water below him rustles with ice
There is frost coming from the ground, in the air mist
All this is pretty, it could not be prettier.

Yes, it could always be prettier, the eye abashes
It is becoming an eye that cannot see enough,
Out of the wood the eye climbs. This is prettier
A field in the evening, tilting up.

The field tilts to the sky. Though it is late
The sky is lighter than the hill field
All this looks easy but really it is extraordinary
Well, it is extraordinary to be so pretty.

And it is careless, and that is always pretty
This field, this owl, this pike, this pool are careless,
As Nature is always careless and indifferent
Who sees, who steps, means nothing, and this is pretty.

So a person can come along like a thief—pretty!—
Stealing a look, pinching the sound and feel,
Lick the icicle broken from the bank
And still say nothing at all, only cry pretty.

Cry pretty, pretty, pretty and you'll be able
Very soon not even to cry pretty
And so be delivered entirely from humanity
This is prettiest of all, it is very pretty.

Watchful

(A Tale of Psyche)

When Watchful came to me he said,
As he never said before,
Wait, wait, I will see you
On Northumberland Moor.

I played with my brothers
In Northumberland House
And we laughed as we skipped and ran
And made a great noise,

And I looked through the window
And saw the sea run white
Against Northumberland,
Country of my delight.

When Watchful spoke,
As he never used to speak,
I drew apart from my brothers,
I scowled to hear Watchful speak,

Come to me, come to me,
Upon Northumberland Moor, hurry!
I will not come yet
But I will come some day.

First, I must play with my brothers
And make some money
On the Stock Exchange. It was funny
How we made so much money
Because we did not want it in the old
Tall house in Northumberland,
In fact we did not want it much at all.

Often we gave parties
In London
For Senior Civil Servants
And barristers
And Junior Members
Of the Government.

I said to my brother Tommy,
It is funny
How they come
When we do not want them very much.

Tommy said, It is funny
Like the money,
We do not want
It or them very much,
Yet they come.

It is funny, Tommy, too, I said,
How the warmth of the parties
Fascinates me, and the wild laughing eyes
Of the people hold me.

You would not have thought
That the people we had
At our parties would have
These wild laughing eyes, but they had.

Watch out, said Tommy, the word is Watchful,
Then
We were in Northumberland again.

The window of our schoolroom was open
And in the group of my brothers in the room was one, quickly,
Who was not a brother, coming to me.

I climbed down from the window in the high moonlight
Along the high brick wall of the kitchen garden
I crawled. But the wall was higher
Than I remembered it was. So when I went to drop
Off the high wall, where we used to by the mulberry tree,
It was suddenly too high, I hung by my fingers above a precipice,
But I could not hang long, I let go, I fell, fell far, fell,
Was caught. I stiffened in the arms that held me,
                                        slipped down and ran free.

Over the saltings I ran. The midnight high wind
Pulled my straight hair in streaks behind me, and I ran and ran
And did not care, as I ran by the sea shore,
If Watchful ran behind or waited for me
On Northumberland Moor.

Oh how strongly the wind drew. When day broke
The waves leapt and their crests ran gold
In the morning sun, the gold sun was in their crests.

Turn away, turn away
From the high crests of the golden sea,
It was funny
How easily I turned away from the high crests, as easily
As from the parties
And the money.

I was running in a wood now, a wood of pine trees,
Very dark it was and silent, I ran on brown pine needles
Silently, and came to a gamekeeper's gallows.
                                    The mournful birds
Hanging there cried: We are not Watchful, and an old badger
Crawling to his sett to die said: I am not Watchful. But the wind
Cried: Hurry! and drove great snowflakes against my face.
Then I came to a dark house and the door swung and I went in,
Oh Watchful, my darling, you have led me such a dance.

He lay on a truckle bed, cold, cold; his eyes shut.

First I made a fire from the wood stacked and the pine cones,
Then I came back to him, Oh Watchful, you are so cold,
So I lay on him to warm him, and by and by
He opened his eyes and laughed to see me cry.

We need not dance any more
He said, Only the fire dances on Northumberland Moor,
The fire you have lighted for me dances
On Northumberland Moor.

Then winter blew away, a sweet sea ran pretty
And in this new world everything was happy.

Piggy to Joey

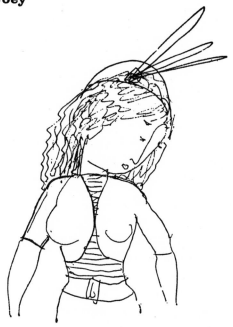

Piggy to Joey,
Piggy to Joe,
Yes, that's what I was—
Piggy to Joe.

Will he come back again?
Oh no, no, no.
Oh how I wish I hadn't been
Piggy to Joe.

But Murderous

A mother slew her unborn babe
In a day of recent date
Because she did not wish him to be born in a world
Of murder and war and hate.
"Oh why should I bear a babe from my womb
To be broke in pieces by a hydrogen bomb?"

I say this woman deserves little pity
That she was a fool and a murderess.
Is a child's destiny to be contained by a mind
That signals only a lady in distress?

And why should *human* infancy be so superior
As to be too good to be born in this world?
Did she think it was an angel or a baa-lamb
That lay in her belly furled?

Oh the child is the young of its species
Alike with that noble, vile, curious and fierce
How foolish this poor mother to suppose
Her act told us aught that was not murderous

(As, item, That the arrogance of a half-baked mind
Breeds murder; makes us all unkind.)

Nodding

Tizdal my beautiful cat
Lies on the old rag mat
In front of the kitchen fire.
Outside the night is black.

The great fat cat
Lies with his paws under him
His whiskers twitch in a dream,
He is slumbering.

The clock on the mantelpiece
Ticks unevenly, tic toc, tic-toc,
Good heavens what is the matter
With the kitchen clock?

Outside an owl hunts,
Hee hee hee hee,
Hunting in the Old Park
From his snowy tree.
What on earth can he find in the park tonight,
It is so wintry?

Now the fire burns suddenly too hot
Tizdal gets up to move,
Why should such an animal
Provoke our love?

The twigs from the elder bush
Are tapping on the window pane
As the wind sets them tapping,
Now the tapping begins again.

One laughs on a night like this
In a room half firelight half dark
With a great lump of a cat
Moving on the hearth,
And the twigs tapping quick,
And the owl in an absolute fit
One laughs supposing creation
Pays for its long plodding
Simply by coming to this—
Cat, night, fire—and a girl nodding.

Widowhood
or The Home-Coming of Lady Ross

(*"Her husband, the Lord of the Isles, is dead, and she lives alone by the sea"*)

Nobody hears me, nobody sees me,
My father, the General, used to say
He had only to come into a room
For everybody else to go out of it.

("Ach, wie schrecklich, so alt zu sein,
   Und diese schrecklichen Tränensäcke,
   Als wenn sie viel geweint hätte!"
Said the young girl to her friend,
In the hotel at Baden.)

My heart is a frozen lump,
I look forward to nothing but Death,
I am glad Harold is not here
To see me now.

("Oh how awful, to be so old,
   And those awful tear-tracks on her cheeks,
   As if she had cried a lot!"
Said the young girl to her friend
In the hotel at Cheltenham.)

Harold loved the hotel at Baden and the hotel at Cheltenham
He loved staying in hotels, he loved staying in 'em.

Now I live alone by the sea
And I am happy as never I used to be,
Harold, can you forgive me?
My family were never much good in company.

That's what you used to say, dear, do you remember,
                                    when I stayed in my room
In the hotel at Baden, or wherever it might be,
                                    Up you would come
Rushing, and kiss me and cry: Rhoda, your family,
I must say, are not much good in company.

Oh Harold, our house looks so beautiful today,
Why did you always want to go away?

The Ass

In the wood of Wallow
Mash, walked Eugenia, a callow
Girl, they said she was,
An ass.

Beyond the wood there lay a soppy mórass
But the path across was firm, was
Not a-wash.

Three years in the wood Eugenia stayed
By briar and bramble and lost ways she was delayed,
And in a witch's house within a thicket of yew trees
Was put to work; but seemed so happy that the witch
Finding no pleasure in her tyranny
Gave her release.
She is an ass, she cried, let her pass
And perish in the soppy mórass.

Eugenia was as happy in the change
To be free to roam and range
As she had been happy and not sad or sorry
At her labours in the witch's bothy.

The sun fell hot upon the causeway
That was not very wide
And the mórass sopped and shuffled
Either side.

And the little beetles ran
About, and all the gnats and the mosquitos sang,
And the mórass was as sweet a green
As Eugenia had ever seen.
She sang: Baa-baa-ba-bay
And seven happy years spent on the way.

Once there came a fiend
Who tempted her to go upon the green
Morass: Come, ass, and go
Upon the green. But she said, No,
She was not such an ass to try the green,
It would deliver her below.

Heigh-ho, heigh-ho,
Never was such a happy idle ass
Since idleness ran glad in Paradise
As Eugenia was.
Paradise. Paradise.

Now the seven years have passed,
The causeway's ended, the soppy mórass
Has sucked its last; the ass
Comes to a sandy pass
Between low sandhills that are tufted over with esparto grass,
Beyond, the great seas splash
And roll in pleasure to be so a-wash,
Their white crests coming at a dash
To fetch the ass.

Oh my poor ass
To run so quickly as if coming home
To where the great waves crash.
Now she is gone. I thought
Into her tomb.

Yet often as I walk that sandy shore
And think the seas
Have long since combed her out that lies
Beneath, I hear the sweet Ass singing still with joy as if
She had won some great prize, as if
All her best wish had come to pass.

The Crown of Bays

They gave him a crown of bays and dressed him up,
But he was listless though famous, he had had enough.
He looked at the audience, They are clapping knaves,
And turning to the Wingèd Form, Who are you? he says.
"I am the Angel of the Considered Bays."
When you go back I will follow you, he said.
"To do that, you must be dead."
I ask it; this people is a basket.

He laid his head in the angel's lap,
Oh let me come with you, let me come.
"Can you say farewell to the people in deep slumbers
Who travel by the Underground railway with happy faces

in numbers?"
These, and these
He said (thinking of the sleepers and the audience) tease,
Let me come with you.
"Only those who expect everything are prepared to take

nothing,"
Said the angel slyly, as posing a conundrum,
"Death may be that."
Still lead; I follow, pat pat.
"Can you say farewell to the Natural Beauties?"
Yes, I look at them through a glass cage, the glaze sullies.

The angel waved a hand and under a tree,
A mighty chestnut whose fine branches
The spring with white flowers enhances,
Lay the bay-crowned Misery.

Oh Angel of Bays, he cries, weeping bitterly,
You have forged a dagger with your visions for my penalty,
Crack my heart, pierce throat, I will come with you,
I only used to think it was worth while living for the view.
How beautiful the sky is that is bright blue
Through the green leaves, and the sun warms
                                      through and through
Before a man hangs they give him what he likes to eat,
So you have given me what I like to see, the trees and no street,
Now to the scaffold, Angel, do your part,
I will come with you. (The angel stabs him to the heart.)

As he lay bleeding his last into the untrod earth
He smiled a happy smile and said:
I had a philosophy of use and wont, it was bad;
I conceded that life was a balance with
Only three ha'pence to the liver's credit,
But to live with three ha'pence was a merit.
I held that nothing to have not wholly bad not wholly good
Was a young man's dream and juvenile aspiration,
Now I am come to that young man's situation,
And expecting everything gladly receive annihilation.

43

"You receive what I do not know,"
Said the angel, and with this word
Flies away and leaves him lying upon the sward.
But over his shoulder airborne came these last words, "Briefly
In my opinion for what it is worth, you die trivially."

Es war einmal

I raised my gun
I took the sight
Against the sun
I shot a kite.

    I raised my gun
    I took the sight
    A second one
    I shot in flight.

        I raised my gun
        I shot a plover
        I loaded up
        And shot another.

            Now round about me
            Lay the dead
            One more, one more,
            Then home to bed.

Pray Heaven, quod I
Send the best
That ever took
Lead to its breast.

Upon the word
Upon the right
Rose up a phoenix
Beaming bright.

I raised my gun
I took the sight
My lead unbarred
That breast of white,

Alas for awful
Magic art
The bullet bounced
Into my heart.

The phoenix bled
My heart cannot
But heavy sits
'Neath leaden shot.

Leave shooting, friend,
Or if you must
Shoot only what
Is mortal dust.

Pray not to Heaven
He stock your bag
Or you may feel
Your vitals sag.

Pray not to Heaven
For heavenly bird
Or Heaven may take you
At your word.

Pretty Baby

Sweet baby, pretty baby, I bless thee,
Thou liest so snug and lookst so prettily,
And yet I think you also look imperially.

Why shouldst thou not? If it is Deity
Couches in mother's lap, prettily, prettily,
Then thou art God and canst not sin or feel guilty,

As we can do, for we have our sins innerly,
Sweet baby. Now I think there is a fee
That you must pay for looking happily

And that is: not to know what being free
From sin means, being sinless. Only we
Can bless and measure that felicity.

But let the angels sing a song for thy birth sweetly,
And we will try to sing songs too, but differently,
For we are earth-born and the song is heavenly.

Is it Happy?

Is it happy for me, is it happy
That my father, Lord Beale, was so famous
And I am a ne'er-do-weel? Is it happy?

And what of my mother—"the lady"
We called her, because she was so high-minded, born Plaidy—
Was it happy for her
That Father was never there?
Was it happy?

And Rory, Rory my brother
Who knew neither father nor brother
Being adopted in infancy by Uncle Pym
Whose name he took, was it happy for him?

Thorwald, our spaniel, gun-trained,
Died of a fatty heart;
Well, Father was never at home,
And I didn't shoot.
Was it happy for Thorwald?

. . . all that money paid out for a worthless scrip
That might have been mine today
If Papa had stuck to Gilt Edged or Blue Chip,
Is that happy?

My father died in his fame
Saving his country and me
From the people over the sea.
How does it feel being Beale,
Lord Beale, and a ne'er-do-weel?

I've brought Mother home to the little house,
Having let the grand one for a commando course,
Telling 'em to look out for the pictures, of course.

All my life I have tried not to be envious
Of Father, or take it out by being nefarious,
Truly I loved him, revere
The memory of this great soldier,
Field Marshall Lord B. he was when he died,
(Happy, for me?)

Mother says I should bring home a bride,
Greatness skips a generation, she says, and he,
My son, need not be a nonentity.

I'll do it, why not?
Play the part out,
Find a sort of happiness in it too I dare say, slyly
Being as it were all this quite so entirely,
Blithely calling the saviour of my country, Father,
(Happy for me)
Blithely begetting sons to carry it farther,
(Will that be?)

I'll ask Cynthia tonight, she'll say yes,
When I've got the Commandos out she'll love the place.

It's occurred to me also once or twice of late
To join the True Church, something Father would hate,
Not the Anglicans of course, they're too humdrum,
It would have to be the Roman Communion.
Well, I've read Father Gerard and about the recusants quite a lot
And can prove: As they *suffered*, there cannot have been
                                        a Catholic Plot.

Is it happy for me, driving Mother mad?
Does she wish I was bad?
Think Rory might have been better than me?
Well, if she does, she don't let me see.

Happy, is it happy?

Hippy-Mo

I had a sweet bird
Called Hippy-Mo
But he did not wish to stay
With me, he wished to go.
Hippy-Mo, Hippy-Mo.

I hugged him tight, I said:
You shall not go,
You shall stay here with me
Hippy-Mo.

Then he grew tall as a house,
Hippy-Mo,
Took me in his claws and would
Not let me go,
Hippy-Mo.

His eyes were black as the night
Through which we flew,
And the lightnings flashed from his eyes
As we flew through,
Hippy-Mo what are
You going to do
With me?

Hippy-Mo, Hippy-Mo,
Brought me to a sunny land,
Put me in a cage
Wherein I rage
And when I rage he holds
My hand
So tight I cannot move
From him,

Hippy-Mo
Let me go,
Do you wish me
To die?

He was so mean he did not condescend
To reply. Even
Yes or no.

The Last Turn of the Screw

I am Miles, I did not die
I only turned, as on shut eye
To feel again the silken dress
Of my lovely governess.

Yes, it was warm, poetical and cosy,
I never saw the other fellow when
I lolled on Lady's lap (I called her Lady)
But there were two of us all right. And both were men.

Yes, there's the oddest part. She made me feel
A hundred years more old than I was, than she was,
She'd had a sheltered life, of course—a vicarage,
Some bustling younger children, a father pious, I'm sure he was.

But two of us? Of me? I'll be explicit,
A soft boy, knowing rather more than boys should, lolling,
No harm in that, on Lady's lap; the other,
Source of my knowledge, half my self by now, but calling . . .

Some children are born innocent, some achieve it,
You scowl; that doesn't fit with your philosophy?
Can you by choosing alter Nature, you inquire?
Yes, my dear sir, you can; I found it fairly easy.

But calling (to go back a step) but calling?—
That proved he was not yet quite One of Us,

The vulgar little beast, the fellow Quint.
It was at first my lordly feelings held him off
That dapper knowingness of his for instance,
The clothes right, being my uncle's, but worn wrong,
The accent careful, well he must be careful,
I dare say he had thumbed a book about it . . .
To spend ten minutes with a Thing like this
Would be too long.
So snobbery made the breach, religion followed . . .
Ten minutes? No, Eternity, with Quint
That Quint, whose seedy sickness in my blood
I could detect (in time?) running to flood,
The sickliness of sin,
Oh yes, I saw quite plain by now
What was going in.
How did I fob him off? (now we know why)
When half my heart
Was panting for him and what he could teach
Reaching for shame, and retching too
(It was, as I have said this squeamishness I had
First judged him bad).

Oh there was still some rotting to go on
In my own heart
Before I was quite ready to cry "Out!"
And see him off, though half my blood went with him.
I grow a shade dramatic here, none went at all,
My sinews have remained the same, my blood, my heart
Have not, as I'm aware, taken a taint,

I was not and I am not now a saint,
But I loved Virtue, and I love her still,
Especially as I see her in the dress
Of my sweetly fatheaded governess . . .
Well, let's be plain, I fobbed Quint off
By simply failing to be clever enough.
By taking nothing in, not looking and not noticing
I made myself as dull to the persuading
Of all that shabby innuendo as
The plainest ten-year schoolboy ever was,
And so I have remained and by intent
Quite dull. And shall remain
Sooner than chance such entering again.

I did not die, but bought my innocence
At the high price of an indifference
Where once I knew the most engaging love
That first through squeamishness made virtue move,
The love, now lost of my sweet governess
Who cannot bear I should be so much less
The Miles she knew, or rather did not know.
Yes, I have lost my interestingness for Lady who,
I fear, like other innocent ladies do,
Hankered for something shady,
Well, say, dramatic, not what I am now,
An empty antic Clumsy, a mere boy.
She'll never know
The strength I have employed and do employ
To make it sure
I shall be this
And nothing more.

I am Miles, I did not die,
I only turn, as on shut eye
To feel again the silken dress
Of my lost and lovely governess,
And sigh and think it strange
That being dull I should feel so much pain.

The Listener

Listening one day on the radio
To "An encounter with mosquitoes in New Guinea"

by Miss Cheeseman,

I fell to thinking of the animal kingdom
And experienced at once a relief of nervous tension.
For I thought, Their battles are as ours, as ours,
They are no different from our own,
Then rose up a Spirit from the ether that touched my eyelids
And cast me in a deep swoon.

How Cruel is the Story of Eve

How cruel is the story of Eve
What responsibility
It has in history
For cruelty.

Touch, where the feeling is most vulnerable,
Unblameworthy—ah reckless—desiring children,
Touch there with a touch of pain?
Abominable.

Ah what cruelty,
In history
What misery.

Put up to barter
The tender feelings
Buy her a husband to rule her
Fool her to marry a master
She must or rue it
The Lord said it.

And man, poor man,
Is he fit to rule,
Pushed to it?
How can he carry it, the governance,
And not suffer for it

Insuffisance?
He must make woman lower then
So he can be higher then.

Oh what cruelty,
In history what misery.

Soon woman grows cunning
Masks her wisdom,
How otherwise will he
Bring food and shelter, kill enemies?
If he did not feel superior
It would be worse for her
And for the tender children
Worse for them.

Oh what cruelty,
In history what misery
Of falsity.

It is only a legend
You say? But what
Is the meaning of the legend
If not
To give blame to women most
And most punishment?

This is the meaning of a legend that colours
All human thought; it is not found among animals.

How cruel is the story of Eve,
What responsibility it has
In history
For misery.

Yet there is this to be said still:
Life would be over long ago
If men and women had not loved each other
Naturally, naturally,
Forgetting their mythology,
They would have died of it else
Long ago, long ago,
And all would be emptiness now
And silence.

Oh dread Nature, for your purpose
To have made them love so.

Oh Grateful Colours, Bright Looks!

The grass is green,
The tulip is red,
A ginger cat walks over
The pink almond petals on the flower bed.
Enough has been said to show
It is life we are talking about. Oh
Grateful colours, bright looks! Well, to go
On. Fabricated things too—front doors and gates,
Bricks, slates, paving stones—are coloured
And as it has been raining and is sunny now
They shine. Only that puddle
Which, reflecting the height of the sky,
Quite gives one a feeling of vertigo, shows
No colour, is a negative. Men!
Seize colours quick, heap them up while you can.
But perhaps it is a false tale that says
The landscape of the dead
Is colourless.

The House of Over-Dew

Over-Dew
Became a dread name for Cynthia
In 1937
It was then that Mr. Minnim first began to talk openly
About his dear wish.
(How dear it was to be
For all of them!)

Mr. and Mrs. Minnim had two sons
Who had done well at school
And won scholarships to Oxford.
Their boyhood was a happy time for all. *Then*
The elder son married Helen,
A fellow-student at the university,
And, coming down, found a good post with sufficient money.
His wife also
Had money of her own. They were doing well.

The younger son, Georgie,
Was engaged to Cynthia. But that did not go so well.
He took a First in Greats, but then
The difficulties began. He could not find a job.
He did nothing, tried again; no good.
He grew sulky. It seemed hopeless.

It was now that the dread name of Over-Dew
Was spoken,
And a scheme bruited. It was this:
The Minnims were sincere and practising Christians.

To Mr. Minnim

Anyone who was not a Christian
Was a half-educated person.
It was, for instance, suggested
That his daughter-in-law should write a *Life of St. Benedict,*
There was no good life of St. Benedict, said Mr. Minnim.
So Cynthia suggested that Helen should write it,
Because Helen was a Mediaeval History student,
Whereas Cynthia herself was a Latinist,
So why not Helen, with her special knowledge?
But Helen was not a Christian,
So, "No," said Mr. Minnim, she was a Half-Educated Person.
The Over-Dew scheme was orthodox Christian.
When Mr. Minnim retired from his accountancy work
He said that they should move from the suburb where they lived
And buy the house of Over-Dew, which was
A retreat for missionaries to have
On their leave-holidays in England.
And now it was being run, he said, in a fantastical fashion.
When they bought it
Everything would be better
And different.

Where was the money to come from? No matter,
They had their savings, also they had the faith
Of Mr. and Mrs. Minnim.

Mrs. Minnim loved her husband
And was pleased to follow him to the ends of the earth,

                                        and certainly

Over-Dew was not that.

But oh when Cynthia heard that word
It was the knell
Of all her life and love. This, she said,
Is the end of happy days and the beginning
Of calamity. Over-Dew, she thought,
Shall be the death of my love and the death of life.
For to that tune, she thought,
Shall come up a European war and personal defeat.

The Georgie situation
Was already sad. What could she do there? Nothing,
But see him and be silent and so enrage,
Or see him and speak, and the more enrage.

The wise and affectionate Cynthia
Must break the engagement and give back the ring.
There is nothing but this that she can do.
She takes up a post at London University
And in lecturing and study passes the days.
No more of that.

She has read a paper to her pupils
And fellow-dons, the subject is
The development of Latin from the first early growth
Upon the Grecian models. The study entrances,
She finds and reads a Latin prayer:

"I devote to Hades and Destruction." It is a prayer
For time of battle, the thought is this:
I dedicate the enemy to Hades and Destruction. And perhaps
One or two of the praying Romans
Will devote also themselves
To Hades and Destruction. Rushing then into battle,
These "devoted" people hope they may be killed. If not,
They are held for dead,
They are stateless, and in religion
Have no part at all. The gods have not accepted them,
They are alive, but yet they are destroyed.
In Cynthia's life, this sad year
Was twice as long as all the happy years before. She must now
Withdraw from Georgie and see him miserable.

She is at work and fast within her family
The happy careless laughter
Of the brothers and sisters
Rings her round,
She has the home tasks, too,
And thinks of Georgie.

At the end of the year, in the bitter snow that fell that Christmas
The phrenzied Minnims
Moved from their life-long suburb.

The house of Over-Dew
Lay buried half in snow
It stood five miles from any town upon a hillside.
Very bleak it was, and all the pipes were froze.
Mrs. Minnim worked hard,

They had a girl to help them then she left.
Mrs. Minnim had courage and was cheerful
But she was by now an old lady. Suddenly
There was the gift of a little money. Mr. Minnim
Bought chasubles for visiting priests. But at first
There were no visitors at all, but only
The old cold house, and the lavatories frozen up
And wood kindling to be chopped and dried.
The work was bitter hard.
Mr. Minnim, released suddenly
From the routine of his accountancy
Suffered in his head a strange numbness,
He moved about in a dream, would take no hand with the dishes.
                                                                Even
When five-and-twenty missionaries came for a conference
He would do nothing.
He paced the garden plots, "and here" he said,
"I will build twelve lavatories. And in this room
We will have a consecration and build an altar."

The thaw came and turned all to mud and slush,
There was still no post for Georgie, he came down from Oxford
And washed the dishes for his mother,
And chopped the wood and moved also in a daze,
The immense learning
Lay off from him, the crude work of the house
Was an excuse from study.

But now Mrs. Minnim was not happy, like a sad animal
She roamed the rooms of Over-Dew. This woman
Who had been so boisterous and so loving

With many friends, but still her own best thoughts
For Mr. Minnim and their sons,
Was like a sad animal that cannot know a reason.
Georgie, with the guilt of the excuse upon his heart,
Grew savage with her. The moody silences
Were shot with cruel words
It was so bitter cold within the house
Though now without the snow was melted and turned to slush.

The money situation preyed upon the mind of Mrs. Minnim.
But her husband
Spoke of faith.

In the suburb where they once lived friends said:
How are the Minnims? Did you hear
That Mr. Minnim had bought chasubles?
And then the foolish, unkind laughter: Chasubles!
It will be
The ruin of them, the end.

There was one hope that Mrs. Minnim had, it was this,
That they might return at last to their house in the suburb,
She had refused to let her husband
Sell this house. No, that she would not allow, No,
That must be for a return.
But now, out of this refusal was made
The bitterness of their life at Over-Dew. For, said her husband,
You kept back the seven hundred and fifty pounds
We might have had for selling the house.

In London
The girl who should have been Georgie's wife
Hears all; understands; loves Georgie; is helpless;

                                                 reads to her class
The Latin prayer: I devote to Hades and Destruction.
She rules the harsh thoughts that run; cries;
Come, love of God.

Anger's Freeing Power

I had a dream three walls stood up wherein a raven bird
Against the walls did beat himself and was not this absurd?

For sun and rain beat in that cell that had its fourth wall free
And daily blew the summer shower and the rain came presently

And all the pretty summer time and all the winter too
That foolish bird did beat himself till he was black and blue.

Rouse up, rouse up, my raven bird, fly by the open wall
You make a prison of a place that is not one at all.

I took my raven by the hand, Oh come, I said, my Raven,
And I will take you by the hand and you shall fly to heaven.

But oh he sobbed and oh he sighed and in a fit he lay
Until two fellow ravens came and stood outside to say:

You wretched bird, conceited lump
You well deserve to pine and thump.

See now a wonder, mark it well
My bird rears up in angry spell,

Oh do I then? he says, and careless flies
O'er flattened wall at once to heaven's skies.

And in my dream I watched him go
And I was glad, I loved him so,

Yet when I woke my eyes were wet
To think Love had not freed my pet

Anger it was that won him hence
As only Anger taught him sense.

Often my tears fall in a shower
Because of Anger's freeing power.

The Castle

I married the Earl of Egremont,
I never saw him by day,
I had him in bed at night,
And cuddled him tight.

We had two boys, twins,
Tommy and Roly,
Roly was so fat
We called him Roly-poly.

Oh that was a romantic time,
The castle had such a lonely look,
The estate,
Heavy with cockle and spurge,
Lay desolate.

The ocean waves
Lapped in the castle caves.

Oh I love the ramshackle castle,
And the room
Where our sons were born.

Oh I love the wild
Parkland,
The mild
Sunshine.

Underneath the wall
Sleeps our pet toad,
There the hollyhocks grow tall.

My children never saw their father,
Do not know,
He sleeps in my arms each night
Till cockcrow.

Oh I love the ramshackle castle,
And the turret room
Where our sons were born.

The Crown of Gold

(An English Writer in Search of an Established English Publisher)

Mother procure for me a golden crown
Said the child, That the fire may not burn me nor the seas drown.

She took the child and ran for three years
                                in the wilderness with him.
And beside them ran a German-Jewish man
And he loved the child and protected him
Crying: Remember Jerusalem.
And he crowned the child with a crown of affection.

But the child said
Mother, it is not a crown of affection I want
It is a crown of gold.

And the child and his mother ran more quickly in the wilderness
And more quickly beside them ran the German-Jewish man
Crying: Remember Jerusalem.
And he said, Nodoby has loved your child as I have loved him.

And the child said, Mother procure for me a crown of gold
You are not required to think about anything else.

And the German-Jewish man kissed the crowned child's hand
                                as he ran
Crying: Remember Jerusalem.

And the child stood in the path
And he took from his head the crown of affection
And threw it at the feet of the German-Jewish man
Crying: Remember Jerusalem.

And they left the German-Jewish man and left the wilderness
And she procured for her child a crown of gold
And they sat in a pleasant garden in a fine city.

And the child said, Mother, gold is the right material for a crown
It is only in the wilderness that crowns of affection are worn,
And she said, No it is not, and began to weep and wring her hands,
Do not be foolish Mother, he said, I am no longer young.
And she said, Remember Jerusalem.

And the wind blew strong and rattled the leaves
                                        of the poplar trees
And the child did not hear, or heard and laughed, he did not care
But the strong wind took the words and carried them
                                        to the wilderness
Where they fell to the ground in a wild place.
And the mother of the child stopped crying and was resigned
                                        to the golden crown
And she said, Now may the fire not burn my child nor
                                        the seas drown.

Our Bog is Dood

Our Bog is dood, our Bog is dood,
They lisped in accents mild,
But when I asked them to explain
They grew a little wild.
How do you know your Bog is dood
My darling little child?

We know because we wish it so
That is enough, they cried,
And straight within each infant eye
Stood up the flame of pride,
And if you do not think it so
You shall be crucified.

Then tell me, darling little ones,
What's dood, suppose Bog is?
Just what we think, the answer came,
Just what we think it is.
They bowed their heads. Our Bog is ours
And we are wholly his.

But when they raised them up again
They had forgotten me
Each one upon each other glared
In pride and misery
For what was dood, and what their Bog
They never could agree.

Oh sweet it was to leave them then,
And sweeter not to see,
And sweetest of all to walk alone
Beside the encroaching sea,
The sea that soon should drown them all,
That never yet drowned me.

The Lady of the Well-Spring

Renoir's "La Source"

He is quite captive to the Lady of the Well-Spring,
Who will rescue him?
Into the French drawing-room the afternoon sun shone
And as the French ladies laughed their white faces
Barred by the balcony shadows seemed to make grimaces.
In a far corner of the room
Sat the English child Joan
As far away as she could get but without exasperation
Only to be freed from the difficulty of conversation
"Quite captive to the lady of the Well-Spring
Who will rescue him?"
Now I have an excuse to go
Said Joan, and walked out of the window
Down the iron staircase and along the path
And then she began to run through the tall wet grass.
Overhead the hot sun slanting
Fell on Joan as she ran through the fields panting,
Faster faster uphill she goes hoping
That as the ground goes uphill steeply sloping
She will find the well-spring. Into a little wood
She runs, the branches catching at her feet draw blood
And there is a sound of piping screaming croaking clacking
As the birds of the wood rise chattering.
And now as she runs there is the bicker
Of a stream growing narrower in a trickle
And a splash and a flinging, it is water springing.
Now with her feet in deep moss Joan stands looking

78

Where on a bank a great white lady is lying
A fair smooth lady whose stomach swelling
Full breasts fine waist and long legs tapering
Are shadowed with grass-green streaks. The lady smiles
Lying naked. The sun stealing
Through the branches, her canopies, glorifies
The beautiful rich fat lady where she lies.
Never before in history
In a place so green and watery
Has lady's flesh and so divine a lady's as this is
With just such an admiring look as Joan's met with.
"Quite captive to the Lady of the Well-Spring?"
What nonsense, it is a thing
French ladies would say
In sophisticated conversation on a warm day.
I do not wish to rescue him, blurts Joan,
The lady lolls, Do you wish to go home?
No, says Joan, I should like to live
Here. Right, says the lady, you are my captive.
The child Joan fully sees the beauty her eye embraces.
Do not think of her as one who loses.

The Wedding Photograph

Goodbye Harry I must have you by me for a time
But once in the jungle you must go off to a higher clime
The old lion on his slow toe
Will eat you up, that is the way you will go.

Oh how I shall like to be alone on the jungle path
But you are all right now for the photograph
So smile Harry smile and I will smile too
Thinking what is going to happen to you,
It is the death wish lights my beautiful eyes
But people think you are lucky to go off with such a pretty prize.
Ah feeble me that only wished alone to roam
Yet dared not without marrying leave home
Ah woe, burn fire, burn in eyes' sheathing
Fan bright fear, fan fire in Harry's breathing.

A House of Mercy

It was a house of female habitation,
Two ladies fair inhabited the house,
And they were brave. For although Fear knocked loud
Upon the door, and said he must come in,
They did not let him in.

There were also two feeble babes, two girls,
That Mrs. S. had by her husband had,
He soon left them and went away to sea,
Nor sent them money, nor came home again
Except to borrow back
Her Naval Officer's Wife's Allowance from Mrs. S.
Who gave it him at once, she thought she should.

There was also the ladies' aunt
And babes' great aunt, a Mrs. Martha Hearn Clode,
And she was elderly.
These ladies put their money all together
And so we lived.

I was the younger of the feeble babes
And when I was a child my mother died
And later Great Aunt Martha Hearn Clode died
And later still my sister went away.

Now I am old I tend my mother's sister
The noble aunt who so long tended us,
Faithful and True her name is. Tranquil.
Also Sardonic. And I tend the house.

It is a house of female habitation,
A house expecting strength as it is strong,
A house of aristocratic mould that looks apart
When tears fall; counts despair
Derisory. Yet it has kept us well. For all its faults,
If they are faults, of sternness and reserve,
It is a Being of warmth I think; at heart
A house of mercy.

Under Wrong Trees . . .
or Freeing the Colonial Peoples

Under wrong trees
Walked the zombies,

They were told to walk under oaks, you know,
But they preferred willows.

It was the first time they had been old
Enough not to do as they were told.

They thus became
Not zombies
But *splendide,*

Until one day they fell in
The river the willows were weeping in,

Which was *stupide*
Of them, people said, and showed they were not old
Enough yet not to do as they were told.

But really I think this tale of wrong trees
Shows that they never were zombies,

But men, women and men.

So why should we notice them?

Egocentric

What care I if good God be
If he be not good to me,
If he will not hear my cry
Nor heed my melancholy midnight sigh?
What care I if he created Lamb,
And golden Lion, and mud-delighting Clam,
And Tiger stepping out on padded toe,
And the fecund earth the Blindworms know?
He made the Sun, the Moon and every Star,
He made the infant Owl and the Baboon,
He made the ruby-orbèd Pelican,
He made all silent inhumanity,
Nescient and quiescent to his will,
Unquickened by the questing conscious flame
That is my glory and my bitter bane.
What care I if Skies are blue,
If God created Gnat and Gnu,
What care I if good God be
If he be not good to me?

Exeat

I remember the Roman Emperor, one of the cruellest of them,
Who used to visit for pleasure his poor prisoners cramped
                                        in dungeons,
So then they would beg him for death, and then he would say:
Oh no, oh no, we are not yet friends enough.
He meant they were not yet friends enough for him
                                        to give them death.
So I fancy my Muse says, when I wish to die,
Oh no, Oh no, we are not yet friends enough,

And Virtue also says:
We are not yet friends enough.

How can a poet commit suicide
When he is still not listening properly to his Muse?
Or a lover of Virtue when
He is always putting her off until tomorrow?

Yet a time may come when a poet or any person
Having a long life behind him, pleasure and sorrow,
But feeble now and expensive to his country
And on the point of no longer being able to make a decision
May fancy Life comes to him with love and says:
We are friends enough now for me to give you death;
Then he may commit suicide, then
He may go.

A Dream of Comparison

(*After reading Book Ten of "Paradise Lost"*)

Two ladies walked on the soft green grass
On the bank of a river by the sea
And one was Mary and the other Eve
And they talked philosophically.

"Oh to be Nothing," said Eve, "oh for a
Cessation of consciousness
With no more impressions beating in
Of various experiences."

"How can Something envisage Nothing?" said Mary,
"Where's your philosophy gone?"
"Storm back through the gates of Birth," cried Eve,
"Where were you before you were born?"

Mary laughed: "I love Life,
I would fight to the death for it,
That's a feeling, you say? I will find
A reason for it."

They walked by the estuary,
Eve and the Virgin Mary,
And they talked until nightfall,
But the difference between them was radical.

O Pug

(to the Brownes' pug dog, on my lap, in their car, coming home from Norfolk)

O Pug, some people do not like you,
But I like you,
Some people say you do not breathe, you snore,
I don't mind,
One person says he is always conscious of your behind,
Is that your fault?

Your own people love you,
All the people in the family that owns you
Love you: Good pug, they cry, Happy pug,
Pug-come-for-a-walk.

You are an old dog now
And in all your life
You have never had cause for a moment's anxiety,
Yet,
In those great eyes of yours,
Those liquid and protuberant orbs,
Lies the shadow of immense insecurity. There
Panic walks.

Yes, yes, I know,
When your mistress is with you,
When your master
Takes you upon his lap,
Just then, for a moment,
Almost you are not frightened,

But at heart you are frightened, you always have been.

O Pug, obstinate old nervous breakdown,
In the midst of *so* much love,
And such comfort,
Still to feel unsafe and be afraid,

How one's heart goes out to you!

Northumberland House

I was always a thoughtful youngster,
Said the lady on the omnibus,
I remember Father used to say:
You are more thoughtful than us.

I was sensitive too, the least thing
Upset me so much,
I used to cry if a fly
Stuck in the hatch.

Mother always said:
Elsie is too good,
There'll never be another like Elsie,
Touch wood.

I liked to be alone
Sitting on the garden path,
My brother said he'd never seen a
Picture more like Faith in the Arena.

They were kindly people, my people,
I could not help being different,
And I think it was good for me
Mixing in a different element.

The poor lady now burst out crying
And I saw her friend was not a friend but a nurse
For she said, Cheer up duckie the next stop is ours,
They got off at Northumberland House.

This great House of the Percys
Is now a lunatic asylum,
But over the gate there still stands
The great Northumberland Lion.

This family animal's tail
Is peculiar in that it is absolutely straight,
And straight as a bar it stood out to drop after them
As they went through the gate.

Mrs Arbuthnot

Mrs Arbuthnot was a poet
A poet of high degree,
But her talent left her;
Now she lives at home by the sea.

In the morning she washes up,
In the afternoon she sleeps,
Only in the evenings sometimes
For her lost talent she weeps,

Crying: I should write a poem,
Can I look a wave in the face
If I do not write a poem about a sea-wave,
Putting the words in place.

Mrs Arbuthnot has died,
She has gone to heaven,
She is one with the heavenly combers now
And need not write about them.

Cry: She is a heavenly comber,
She runs with a comb of fire,
Nobody writes or wishes to
Who is one with their desire.

Dear Child of God

Dear child of God
With the tears on your face
And your hands clasped in anger
What is the matter with your race?

In the beginning, Father,
You made the terms of our survival
That we should use our intelligence
To kill every rival.

The poison of this ferocity
Runs in our nature,
And O Lord thou knowest
How it nourishes thy creatures.

Oh what a lively poison it was
To bring us to full growth,
Is then becoming loving
As much as our life is worth?

It is a price I would pay
To grow loving and kind,
The price of my life
And the life of human kind.

Father in heaven
Dear Father of peacefulness
It is not often we remember
You put this poison in us,

Generally we stand
With the tears on our face
And our hands clasped in anger,
Faithful but unfortunate.

I had a dream . . .

I had a dream I was Helen of Troy
In looks, age and circumstance,
But otherwise I was myself.

It was the ninth year of the siege
And I did not love anybody very much
Except perhaps Cassandra,
It was those peculiar eyes she had
As if she were short-sighted
That made me feel I could talk to her,
I would have loved anybody I could talk to.
I suppose you know how it's going to end, I said,
As well as I do? Dreams, dreams? They aren't dreams
You know. Do you know?

I used to walk on the walls
And look towards the Grecian tents . . .
It's odd, I said (to Cassandra, of course) how
Everything one has ever read about Troy
As they have always been such splendid writers who were writing
Naturally gets into one's conversation . . .
Where Cressid lay that night, except they did not say
How beastly Scamander looks under this sort of sky,
And the black Greek ships piled up on the seashore beyond
Like prison hulks, like slugs. So there we were
On the walls of Troy. But what I did not know,
And I could not get Cassandra to say either,
Was which of the Helen legends I was,
The phantom, with the real Helen in Egypt,
Or the flesh-and-blood one here
That Menelaus would take back to Sparta.

Remembering this, that there was still some uncertainty,
Raised my spirits. I must say
Dispiritedness was what we were all sunk in,
And though the Royal Family may have seemed spectral
Their dispiritedness was substantial enough, and I dare say
The Greeks were in much the same case, dispirited;
Well, nine years there had been of it, and now
The heavy weather, and the smells
From the battlefield, when the wind was in that direction,
And the spirit of the men, too, on both sides,
This was substantial enough; it seemed to me
Like the spirit of all armies, on all plains, in all wars, the men
No longer thinking why they were there
Or caring, but going on; like the song the English used to sing

In the first world war: We're here because, we're here because,
We're here because, we're here. This was the only time
I heard Cassandra laugh, when I sung this to her. I said:
There you are, you laugh; that shows you are not nearly so
Religious as you think. That's blasphemous, that laugh,
Sets you free. But then she got frightened. All right, I said,
Don't be free, go along and finish up

                         on Clytemnestra's sword-point,
Pinked like a good girl. I used to get so cross.
Paris was stupid, it was impossible to talk to him.
Hector might have been different, at least he understood enough
To be offended—fear of the gods again, I suppose—because
When I said: Well, you know what the Trojan Women
Are going to say about the sack of Troy and being led away
Into captivity, they are going to say: If these things
Had not happened to us we should not be remembered.

                                    I hope that
Will be a comfort to you. He was angry and said
I should bring ill luck to Troy by my impiety, so I laughed
But I felt more like crying. I went into our palace then
And into my own room. But the heaviness of the sky
Still oppressed me, and the sad colours of rust and blood
I saw everywhere, as Cassandra saw too. Oh, I thought,
It is an ominous eternal moment I am captive in, it is always
This heavy weather, these colours, and the smell of the dead men.
It is curious to be caught in a moment of pause like this,
As a river pauses before it plunges in a great waterfall.
I was at home with these people at least in this, that we wished
It was over and done with. But oh, Cassandra, I said,

                               catching hold of her,
For she was running away, I shall never make

That mischievous laughing Helen, who goes home with Menelaus
And over her needlework, in the quiet palace, laughs,
Telling her story, and cries: Oh shameful me. I am only at home
In this moment of pause, where feelings, colours and spirits

are substantial,

But people are ghosts. When the pause finishes
I shall wake.